THE DREAM WEAVER'S GUIDE

DECODING THE LANGUAGE OF DREAMS

DR. MINAKSHI BANSAL

DEDICATION

To all the dreamers who dare to explore the depths of their subconscious and to those who seek to unravel the mysteries of the night. May your dreams guide you on your path towards self-discovery, healing, and a more meaningful life.

ᗐᗐᗐ

Contents

Prayer   *ix*

About The Author   *xi*

Preface   *xv*

1. Your Nightly Stories: Unraveling The Mysteries Of Dreams.   1

Part 1

2. Dream Decoder: A Simple Guide To Understanding Your Dreams   7

Part 2

3. The Dream Dictionary: What Your Dreams Are Trying To Tell You.   13

Part 3

4. Messages From The Subconscious: Unlocking The Secrets Of Your Dreams.   19

Part 4

5. Dream Wisdom: Tap Into The Hidden Messages Of Your Dreams.   25

Part 5

6. The Dreamer's Handbook: Your Guide To Interpreting Dreams.   31

Part 6

7. Nightly Adventures: Exploring The World Of Your Dreams.   37

Part 7

8. The Dream Weaver's Toolkit: Tools For Understanding Your Dreams.   43

Part 8

9. Beyond Reality: Journeying Through The Landscape Of Your Dreams.   49

Contents

Part 9

10. The Dreamer's Journal: A Guide To Recording And Interpreting Your Dreams.   55

Part 10

11. Whispers Of The Night: Deciphering The Language Of Dreams.   61

Part 11

12. From Slumber To Insight: Discovering The Meaning Of Your Dreams.   67

Part 12

13. The Dream Oracle: Using Your Dreams For Guidance And Insight.   73

Part 13

14. Dreamscape: Navigating The World Of Your Dreams.   79

Part 14

15. The Power Of Dreams: Unlocking The Potential Of Your Dreams.   85

Part 15

16. Dream Alchemy: Transforming Your Dreams Into Wisdom.   91

Part 16

17. The Dreamer's Compass: Using Your Dreams To Find Your Way.   97

Part 17

18. The Art Of Dreaming: Cultivating A Rich Dream Life.   103

Part 18

19. The Dream Therapist: Using Your Dreams For Healing And   109

Contents

Growth.

Part 19

20. The Lucid Dreamer: Awakening To Your Dreams.   115

Part 20

21. SUMMARY   121

Citation and References   125

Other Books of the Author   127

CONTACT   133

Prayer

"Om Bhadram Karnebhih Shrinuyama Devah

Bhadram Pashyemakshabhiryajatrah

Sthirairangais Tushtuvamsastanubhih

Vyashema Devahitam Yadayuh

Svasti Na Indro Vriddhashravah

Svasti Nah Pusha Vishwavedah

Svasti Nastarkshyo Arishtanemih

Svasti No Brihaspatir Dadhatu

Om Shantih Shantih Shantih"

This mantra is a prayer for universal well-being, invoking the blessings of various deities for protection, health, and happiness. It emphasizes the importance of experiencing the auspicious through all senses and living a life aligned with divine purpose. The repetition of "Shantih" at the end signifies a deep desire for peace in the individual, the environment, and the universe at large. This mantra is often recited as a prayer for peace, prosperity, and the physical and spiritual well-being of all beings.

▷▷▷

About The Author

This book represents the culmination of extensive research and meticulous analysis, incorporating a diverse range of sources, including numerous books, scholarly studies, and personal experiences. Additionally, I have scoured various websites to gather relevant information and data essential for the compilation of this work. I have taken every precaution to ensure the accuracy of the information presented and have diligently cited all sources to acknowledge their contributions.

From her earliest days, Minakshi was distinguished by an insatiable appetite for reading. Her literary universe was inhabited by characters and narratives that spanned ethical tales, motivational and inspirational stories, and the mythic parables imbued with life lessons. This voracious reading habit was not merely for personal edification but was driven by a desire to distill and disseminate the essence of these narratives to foster the development of students and peers alike. She was particularly captivated by the lives and teachings of historical figures and spiritual leaders such as Adi Shankaracharya, Swami Vivekananda, Dr. APJ Abdul Kalam, Mahamana Pandit Madan Mohan Malviya, Mahatma Gandhi, Sardar Vallabhai Patel, and Vinoba Bhave, among others. Their philosophies and life stories fueled her ambition to embody their ideals of resilience, selflessness, and relentless pursuit of knowledge.

Dr. Minakshi's academic and practical engagement with psychology has been equally noteworthy. As a research scholar, her focus has been on exploring the intricate tapestry of the human psyche, aiming to unlock the potential for psychological well-being and societal harmony. Her scholarly work is complemented by her active involvement in social work, where she employs her academic insights to make tangible differences in the lives of the underprivileged. Her endeavours in social work are characterized by an innovative approach that combines traditional wisdom with contemporary psychological practices to address the multifaceted challenges faced by these communities.

Her artistic talents, another facet of her diverse capabilities, are not merely a personal passion but also serve as a medium through which she communicates and connects with others. Her art, rich in symbolism and emotional depth, reflects her philosophical inquiries and social concerns, offering viewers a glimpse into the breadth of her intellect and the depth of her compassion.

In addition to her contributions to the arts and social sciences, Dr. Minakshi has embraced the healing arts of Pranic Healing, mastering the techniques developed by Master Choa Kok Sui. This practice, which focuses on the manipulation of Prana or life energy to heal the body and aura, has been both a personal journey of discovery and a means through which she extends her healing touch to others. Her proficiency in Pranic Healing is complemented by her advocacy and teaching of various forms of meditation aimed at rejuvenation, personal betterment, and the cultivation of harmony within individuals and communities alike.

Dr. Minakshi's life is a narrative of relentless pursuit, not just of personal achievement but of the upliftment and empowerment of society at large. Her diverse interests and talents—spanning the arts, literature, psychology, and the healing practices—converge on a singular path of service. She embodies the spirit of the luminaries who inspired her, channelling their legacy through her actions and teachings. Through her books, art, and social initiatives, she continues to inspire a new generation to embark on their own journeys of self-discovery, resilience, and altruism.

Her commitment to social betterment, particularly her focus on uplifting underprivileged children, reflects a deep understanding of the transformative potential of education and personal development. By integrating her knowledge of psychology, her artistic sensibilities, and her healing practices, Dr. Bansal has developed a holistic approach to social work that addresses both the immediate needs and the long-term well-being of the communities she serves.

As an author, Dr. Minakshi's writings offer a blend of inspirational insights, practical wisdom, and reflective contemplations drawn from her extensive reading and life experiences. Her books serve as a guide for those seeking to navigate the complexities of life with grace, resilience, and purpose. Through her narratives, she extends an invitation to her readers to explore the depths of their own potential and to contribute meaningfully to the collective well-being of society.

In Dr. Minakshi Bansal, we find a remarkable synthesis of the artist, the scholar, the healer, and the social activist. Her life's work stands as a beacon of hope and a source of inspiration for individuals seeking to make a difference in the world. Her story is a compelling reminder of the power of individual action, rooted in compassion and driven by a profound commitment to the betterment of humanity. Dr. Minakshi's legacy is not just in the tangible outcomes of her efforts but in the enduring spirit of inquiry, empathy, and service that she embodies.

ppp

Preface

In the tapestry of human experience, dreams have long been a source of fascination, wonder, and perplexity. From the earliest whispers of civilization to the modern age of science, dreams have woven their way into our stories, our art, and our understanding of ourselves. They are the nocturnal dance of our subconscious, a kaleidoscope of images, emotions, and sensations that often defy logic and reason. Yet, within their seemingly chaotic nature lies a profound language, a language that, once deciphered, can offer invaluable insights into the depths of our being.

In this book, I invite you to embark on a journey of exploration and self-discovery into this enigmatic world of dreams. I have spent a lifetime delving into the mysteries of the subconscious, seeking to understand the hidden messages that our dreams whisper to us in the quiet hours of the night. Through personal experience, extensive research, and the guidance of countless dreamers who have shared their stories with me, I have come to believe that dreams are not merely fleeting illusions, but rather a profound source of wisdom, healing, and personal growth.

In this book, you will find a comprehensive guide to understanding and interpreting your dreams. We will explore the rich history of dream interpretation, tracing its roots through ancient civilizations and spiritual traditions. We will delve into the symbolism of common dream themes, from flying and falling to being chased and appearing naked in public. We will examine the role of emotions in our dreams and how they can reflect our underlying feelings and attitudes.

We will also explore various techniques for interpreting dreams, including dream journaling, dream incubation, and lucid dreaming. We will discuss the importance of creating a dream-friendly environment, paying attention to our sleep hygiene, and seeking guidance from trusted friends, therapists, or dream interpreters.

Throughout this book, I will share personal anecdotes and case studies that illustrate the transformative power of dreams. You will hear from people who have used their dreams to overcome fears, heal from trauma, and find their true purpose in life. You will also discover how dreams can spark creativity, inspire innovation, and guide us towards a more fulfilling and meaningful existence.

This book is not a definitive guide to dream interpretation. There is no one-size-fits-all approach to understanding the language of dreams, as each individual's dream world is as unique as their fingerprint. However, by sharing the tools and knowledge I have acquired over the years, I hope to empower you to embark on your own journey of dream exploration and self-discovery.

I believe that dreams are a gift, a portal to a realm where anything is possible. By embracing our dreams, we open ourselves to a world of infinite possibilities. We learn to trust our intuition, confront our fears, and tap into our hidden potential. We discover that our dreams are not merely fleeting illusions, but a profound language that speaks to the very core of our being.

It is my sincere hope that this book will serve as a guide and inspiration for all who seek to understand the mysteries of their dreams. May it empower you to awaken to the hidden wisdom that lies within your slumbering mind and to embark on a journey of self-discovery that will enrich your life in countless ways.

Dr. Minakshi Bansal
Social Activist
Ahmedabad, Gujarat, Bharat

🙏🙏🙏

ONE

Your Nightly Stories: Unraveling the Mysteries of Dreams.

———❦———

Dreams, those enigmatic narratives that unfold in the theater of our sleeping minds, have captivated and perplexed humanity since time immemorial. They are the kaleidoscopic fragments of our subconscious, woven together into a tapestry of images, emotions, and sensations that often defy logic and reason. For centuries, dreams have been regarded as portals to the divine, messages from the spirit world, or mere random firings of neurons. Yet, beneath their seemingly chaotic nature lies a profound language that, once deciphered, can offer invaluable insights into our deepest selves.

In this exploration of dreams, we embark on a journey to unravel the mysteries that shroud these nightly stories. We delve into the rich history of dream interpretation, tracing its roots through ancient civilizations and spiritual traditions. From the dream temples of ancient Greece to the shamanic rituals of indigenous cultures, dreams have been revered as a source of wisdom, guidance, and prophecy. They have been seen as a means of communicating with ancestors, deities, and the collective unconscious.

The scientific study of dreams, known as oneirology, emerged in the late 19th century with the pioneering work of Sigmund Freud. Freud proposed that dreams were the "royal road to the unconscious," a window into our repressed desires, fears, and conflicts. He believed that dreams were symbolic representations of our hidden motivations, often disguised in bizarre and seemingly nonsensical forms. While Freud's theories have been challenged and refined over the years, his work laid the foundation for modern dream research.

Today, scientists recognize that dreams are a complex phenomenon with multiple functions. They are believed to play a role in memory consolidation, emotional regulation, problem-solving, and creativity. Dreams may also serve as a virtual reality simulator, allowing us to practice skills and confront fears in a safe environment. However, the precise mechanisms underlying dream generation and their meaning remain elusive.

One of the most intriguing aspects of dreams is their symbolic nature. Dreams often employ metaphors, allegories, and puns to convey their messages. They may draw upon personal experiences, cultural symbols, and archetypal imagery. Understanding the language of dreams requires a willingness to explore the depths of our own psyche and to consider the broader context in which our dreams occur.

Common dream themes, such as flying, falling, being chased, or appearing naked in public, often have universal interpretations.

Flying dreams, for example, may symbolize a sense of freedom, liberation, or ambition. Falling dreams may represent insecurity, vulnerability, or a fear of failure. Being chased dreams may reflect feelings of anxiety, guilt, or unresolved conflict. Appearing naked dreams may signify a fear of exposure, vulnerability, or a desire for authenticity.

However, it's important to note that dream interpretation is a highly personal and subjective process. The same dream symbol can have different meanings for different people, depending on their individual experiences, beliefs, and associations. A snake, for instance, may represent danger and temptation for one person, while it may symbolize healing and transformation for another.

To unlock the meaning of our dreams, we must engage in a dialogue with our subconscious. This involves paying attention to the details of our dreams, exploring our emotional responses, and considering the broader context of our waking lives. Dream journaling is a valuable tool for this process, as it allows us to capture the fleeting images and emotions of our dreams before they fade from memory. By reviewing our dream journal entries over time, we may begin to notice patterns, recurring themes, and personal symbols that shed light on our inner world.

In addition to personal reflection, there are many resources available to help us interpret our dreams. Dream dictionaries, online forums, and professional dream interpreters can offer valuable insights and guidance. However, it's important to approach these resources with a critical eye and to trust our own intuition. Ultimately, the most meaningful interpretations of our dreams come from within.

By embracing our dreams as a source of wisdom, creativity, and self-discovery, we open ourselves to a world of infinite possibilities. We learn to trust our intuition, confront our fears, and integrate the disparate parts of ourselves. We discover that our dreams are not merely random firings of neurons, but a profound language that speaks to the very core of our being. By learning to listen to this language, we can awaken to a deeper understanding of ourselves and our place in the universe.

ϷϷϷ

Dreams are not mere illusions that vanish with the morning light. They are a secret language whispered by the subconscious, waiting to be deciphered. Listen closely, for within their cryptic messages lie profound truths about yourself and your life's journey.

TWO

DREAM DECODER: A SIMPLE GUIDE TO UNDERSTANDING YOUR DREAMS

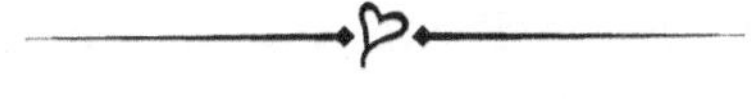

Dreams are a fascinating and often bewildering aspect of the human experience. They can be vivid, emotional, and seemingly nonsensical, leaving us with a sense of wonder and curiosity upon waking. But what do these nightly stories mean? Are they mere random firings of neurons, or do they hold deeper significance? This simple guide aims to provide you with the tools and understanding to decode your dreams and unlock the messages hidden within.

First and foremost, it is essential to recognize that dreams are highly personal and subjective. There is no one-size-fits-all interpretation for any given dream symbol or theme. The meaning of a dream can vary greatly depending on the individual's personal experiences, cultural background, beliefs, and emotional state. Therefore, the most effective approach to dream decoding is to cultivate a deep understanding of your own unique dream language.

To begin this journey of self-discovery, start by keeping a dream journal. Place a notebook and pen by your bedside and make it a habit to jot down your dreams as soon as you wake up, even if you only remember fragments or fleeting images. Over time, patterns and recurring symbols will emerge, revealing valuable insights into your subconscious mind.

As you record your dreams, pay attention to the emotions you experienced during the dream. Were you happy, sad, scared, or angry? These emotions can provide important clues about the underlying meaning of the dream. For example, a recurring dream of being chased may indicate feelings of anxiety or unresolved conflict in your waking life.

Next, consider the context of the dream. What were the people, places, and objects that appeared in your dream? How did they interact with each other and with you? The context can shed light on the symbolism of the dream. For instance, a dream about your childhood home may symbolize a longing for the past or a desire to reconnect with your roots.

Once you have gathered this information, you can begin to explore the symbolism of your dreams. There are many resources available to help you with this process, including dream dictionaries, online forums, and professional dream interpreters. However, it is important to remember that these resources should be used as a starting point for your own personal exploration. The most meaningful interpretations will come from your own intuition and understanding of your unique dream language.

Some common dream symbols and their potential meanings include:

Water: Often represents emotions, the unconscious mind, or the flow of life.

Flying: Can symbolize freedom, ambition, or spiritual transcendence.

Falling: May indicate insecurity, vulnerability, or a fear of failure.

Being chased: Can reflect feelings of anxiety, guilt, or unresolved conflict.

Animals: Often represent instincts, primal urges, or aspects of your personality.

Death: Can symbolize endings, transformations, or the need to let go.

Nudity: May represent vulnerability, shame, or a desire for authenticity.

However, these are just general interpretations. The true meaning of a symbol in your dream will depend on your personal associations and the context of the dream. For example, a snake may represent danger and temptation for one person, while it may symbolize healing and transformation for another.

As you delve deeper into your dreams, you may discover recurring themes that reflect your core values, beliefs, and aspirations. These themes can provide valuable guidance and direction in your waking life. For instance, if you frequently dream about helping others, it may indicate a strong desire to make a positive impact on the world.

Dream decoding is not an exact science, but rather an ongoing process of self-discovery. By paying attention to your dreams, exploring their symbolism, and integrating their messages into your waking life, you can unlock their hidden wisdom and potential. Remember, your dreams are a unique and powerful tool for personal growth and transformation. Embrace them with curiosity, openness, and a willingness to learn, and they will reward you with invaluable insights into your deepest self.

In addition to the above, here are some additional tips for decoding your dreams:

Look for puns and wordplay: Dreams often use puns and wordplay to convey their messages. For example, a dream about a broken heart may not be about romantic heartbreak, but rather about a feeling of emotional brokenness.

Consider the dream's overall mood: The overall mood of a dream can provide important clues about its meaning. For example, a happy dream may be a sign that you are on the right track in your life, while a sad dream may be a warning that you need to make some changes.

Talk to a trusted friend or therapist: If you are struggling to understand a dream, talking to a trusted friend or therapist can be helpful. They can offer a different perspective and help you to see things that you may have missed.

Remember, dream decoding is a journey, not a destination. There is always more to learn and discover about yourself through your dreams. By embracing your dreams with curiosity and openness, you can unlock their hidden wisdom and potential.

ᐅᐅᐅ

Imagine your dreams as a treasure map, filled with symbols and metaphors guiding you towards hidden riches. Each dream is a clue, a piece of the puzzle that reveals your deepest desires, fears, and untapped potential.

THREE

THE DREAM DICTIONARY: WHAT YOUR DREAMS ARE TRYING TO TELL YOU.

Dreams have fascinated and perplexed humanity for centuries. They are a nightly journey into the mysterious realm of the subconscious, where logic and reason often take a back seat to symbolism and metaphor. While the exact meaning of dreams remains a topic of debate among scientists and psychologists, there is no denying that they hold a wealth of information about our inner selves. Like a secret language, dreams communicate with us through a rich tapestry of images, emotions, and sensations. Understanding this language can provide valuable insights into our deepest desires, fears, and unresolved conflicts.

The Dream Dictionary serves as a guide to deciphering this language. It is a compilation of common dream symbols and their potential meanings, based on centuries of dream interpretation and modern psychological research. However, it is important to remember that dream interpretation is not an exact science. The same symbol can have different meanings for different people, depending on their personal experiences, cultural background, and emotional state. Therefore, the Dream Dictionary should be used as a starting point for your own personal exploration and understanding of your dreams.

One of the most common dream symbols is water. Water often represents our emotions and the unconscious mind. Dreaming of calm water may symbolize peace and tranquility, while turbulent water may indicate emotional turmoil or unresolved conflicts. Water can also represent the flow of life, with rivers symbolizing the journey of life and oceans representing the vastness of the unknown.

Another common dream symbol is flying. Flying dreams often evoke feelings of freedom, liberation, and empowerment. They can represent a desire to escape from limitations or to soar above challenges. Flying dreams can also symbolize spiritual transcendence or a connection to the divine.

Falling is a common dream theme that often elicits feelings of fear and anxiety. Falling dreams may represent a loss of control, insecurity, or a fear of failure. They can also symbolize a need to let go of something or to surrender to a higher power.

Being chased is another common dream theme that can be quite unsettling. Being chased dreams often represent feelings of anxiety, guilt, or unresolved conflict. The chaser can be a person, animal, or even a monster, symbolizing something that we are trying to avoid or confront.

Animals are frequent visitors in our dreams, and they often carry symbolic meaning. The type of animal and its behavior in the dream can provide clues to its interpretation. For example, a snake may represent danger or temptation, while a dog may symbolize loyalty and protection. Animals can also represent different aspects of our own personality, with a lion symbolizing courage and a fox symbolizing cunning.

Death is a powerful dream symbol that can be both frightening and enlightening. Dreaming of death does not necessarily predict an actual death, but rather represents endings, transformations, or the need to let go of something. Death dreams can also symbolize a fear of the unknown or a desire for rebirth.

Nudity is a common dream theme that can evoke feelings of vulnerability, shame, or exposure. Nudity dreams may represent a fear of being judged or a desire for authenticity. They can also symbolize a need to shed old habits or beliefs and embrace a new identity.

These are just a few examples of common dream symbols and their potential meanings. The Dream Dictionary is a vast and ever-evolving resource that can help you unlock the hidden messages of your dreams. By exploring the symbolism of your dreams and reflecting on their personal significance, you can gain valuable insights into your innermost self and your journey through life.

Remember, dream interpretation is a personal and subjective process. There is no right or wrong way to interpret a dream. The most important thing is to be open to the messages that your dreams are trying to convey. By paying attention to your dreams and exploring their meaning, you can gain a deeper understanding of yourself and your place in the world.

ᗆᗆᗆ

The dreamscape is a vast and ever-changing landscape, a mirror reflecting your inner world. Explore its hidden corners, embrace its unexpected twists and turns, and uncover the treasures that lie within its depths.

FOUR

MESSAGES FROM THE SUBCONSCIOUS: UNLOCKING THE SECRETS OF YOUR DREAMS.

Dreams have long been a source of fascination and intrigue, serving as a bridge between our conscious and subconscious minds. They are the whispers of our inner selves, offering a glimpse into the hidden depths of our emotions, desires, and fears. Understanding these messages from the subconscious can unlock a treasure trove of self-awareness and personal growth.

Throughout history, dreams have been interpreted as omens, prophecies, and divine messages. Ancient civilizations, such as the Egyptians and Greeks, believed that dreams were a direct line of communication with the gods. They built elaborate dream temples and consulted dream interpreters to decipher the hidden meanings within their nightly visions. While modern science has offered a more rational understanding of dreams, their significance and potential for self-discovery remain undeniable.

Dreams are a reflection of our subconscious mind, a vast reservoir of thoughts, feelings, and experiences that lie beneath the surface of our conscious awareness. This hidden realm is constantly processing information, sorting through memories, and making connections that our waking minds may not perceive. Dreams provide a unique opportunity to tap into this vast storehouse of knowledge and gain a deeper understanding of ourselves.

One of the primary ways that dreams communicate with us is through symbolism. Dreams rarely present literal representations of our waking lives, but instead use metaphors, allegories, and archetypes to convey their messages. Common dream symbols, such as water, flying, falling, and being chased, often carry universal meanings that resonate with people across cultures and time periods. However, the interpretation of these symbols can also be highly personal, depending on the individual's unique experiences and associations.

For example, water in a dream may represent emotions, the unconscious mind, or the flow of life. Dreaming of calm water may symbolize peace and tranquility, while turbulent water may indicate emotional turmoil or unresolved conflicts. Similarly, flying dreams often evoke feelings of freedom, liberation, and empowerment, while falling dreams may represent insecurity, vulnerability, or a fear of failure.

By paying attention to the symbols and themes that appear in our dreams, we can begin to decipher the messages that our subconscious is trying to convey. A recurring dream of being chased, for example, may indicate a need to confront a fear or anxiety in our waking life. A dream of flying may signify a desire for more freedom or independence. By exploring the meaning of these symbols, we can gain valuable insights into our deepest desires, fears, and unresolved conflicts.

Another way that dreams communicate with us is through emotions. Dreams can evoke a wide range of emotions, from joy and excitement to fear and anger. These emotions often reflect our underlying feelings about the events and situations depicted in the dream. For instance, a dream about a loved one may evoke feelings of happiness and nostalgia, while a dream about a traumatic event may trigger feelings of fear and anxiety.

By paying attention to the emotions we experience in our dreams, we can gain a deeper understanding of our emotional landscape. We may discover hidden anxieties, suppressed desires, or unresolved conflicts that are influencing our waking lives. Dreams can also serve as a cathartic release for pent-up emotions, allowing us to process difficult experiences and move forward.

Dream interpretation is a personal and subjective process. There is no one-size-fits-all approach to decoding the messages of our dreams. However, there are several tools and techniques that can help us unlock their hidden meanings.

Keeping a dream journal is a powerful tool for dream interpretation. By recording our dreams as soon as we wake up, we can capture the details and emotions before they fade from memory. Over time, patterns and recurring themes may emerge, revealing valuable insights into our subconscious mind.

Another helpful technique is to share our dreams with a trusted friend, therapist, or dream interpreter. Discussing our dreams with others can provide new perspectives and interpretations that we may not have considered on our own.

Ultimately, the most effective way to unlock the secrets of our dreams is to approach them with curiosity, openness, and a willingness to explore the depths of our own psyche. By paying attention to the symbols, emotions, and themes that appear in our dreams, we can gain valuable insights into our innermost selves and our journey through life. Dreams are a gift from our subconscious, offering us a window into the hidden workings of our minds. By learning to decipher their messages, we can awaken to a deeper understanding of ourselves and our place in the world.

ϸϸϸ

Dream journaling is like planting seeds of self-discovery. With each entry, you nurture a garden of insights, watching as the patterns and themes of your subconscious mind blossom into greater understanding.

FIVE

DREAM WISDOM: TAP INTO THE HIDDEN MESSAGES OF YOUR DREAMS.

In the hush of slumber, when the world retreats and our conscious minds release their grip on reality, a hidden world awakens within us. It's a realm where the ordinary transforms into the extraordinary, where the mundane becomes symbolic, and where our deepest fears and desires are laid bare. This is the world of dreams, a landscape rich with metaphors, emotions, and intuitive insights. To truly understand ourselves and our place in the universe, we must learn to tap into the wisdom that resides within these nightly narratives.

Dreams have been a source of fascination and intrigue for millennia. Ancient civilizations revered dreams as messages from the gods, while modern psychologists view them as a window into the subconscious mind. Regardless of their origin or purpose, dreams hold a wealth of information about our inner selves. They can reveal our hidden fears and anxieties, illuminate our deepest desires, and offer guidance on our life path.

The language of dreams is often symbolic and metaphorical. It's a language that speaks to us through images, emotions, and sensations, rather than words. To decipher this language, we must learn to listen with our hearts and minds, to pay attention to the subtle nuances of our dreams, and to trust our intuition.

One of the most common ways that dreams communicate with us is through recurring symbols. These symbols may appear in different forms and contexts, but they often carry a consistent message. For example, water may symbolize our emotions, with calm water representing peace and tranquility, while turbulent water may indicate emotional turmoil. Animals often appear in dreams as symbols of our instincts and primal urges, while houses and buildings may represent different aspects of our personality.

Another way that dreams communicate with us is through emotions. Dreams can evoke a wide range of emotions, from joy and excitement to fear and anger. These emotions often reflect our underlying feelings about the events and situations depicted in the dream. For instance, a dream about a loved one may evoke feelings of happiness and nostalgia, while a dream about a traumatic event may trigger feelings of fear and anxiety.

By paying attention to the symbols and emotions that appear in our dreams, we can begin to uncover their hidden messages. We may discover recurring themes that reflect our core values, beliefs, and aspirations. We may also gain insights into our relationships, career choices, and personal struggles.

Dream journaling is a powerful tool for tapping into the wisdom of our dreams. By recording our dreams as soon as we wake up, we can capture the details and emotions before they fade from memory. Over time, patterns and recurring themes may emerge, revealing valuable insights into our subconscious mind.

Dream journaling can also help us to identify and address recurring nightmares. By understanding the underlying fears and anxieties that fuel our nightmares, we can begin to heal and transform them.

Sharing our dreams with others can also be a valuable way to gain new perspectives and insights. Talking to a trusted friend, therapist, or dream interpreter can help us to make sense of our dreams and uncover their hidden meanings.

In addition to these techniques, there are many other ways to tap into the wisdom of our dreams. We can practice lucid dreaming, where we become aware that we are dreaming and can consciously influence the dream narrative. We can also explore dream incubation, where we set an intention before bed to dream about a specific topic or issue.

Ultimately, the key to tapping into the wisdom of our dreams is to approach them with curiosity, openness, and a willingness to learn. By embracing our dreams as a source of guidance and self-discovery, we can unlock their hidden potential and transform our lives.

Dreams are a powerful tool for personal growth and transformation. They offer us a unique opportunity to explore the depths of our subconscious mind, to confront our fears and anxieties, and to gain a deeper understanding of ourselves and our place in the world. By tapping into the wisdom of our dreams, we can unlock a world of infinite possibilities and awaken to a life of greater meaning, purpose, and fulfillment.

ᘐᘐᘐ

Don't dismiss your dreams as mere fantasies; they are a potent source of wisdom and guidance. Just as a compass points towards true north, your dreams can guide you towards your true purpose and passions.

SIX

THE DREAMER'S HANDBOOK: YOUR GUIDE TO INTERPRETING DREAMS.

Dreams, those enigmatic tapestries woven in the loom of our sleeping minds, have been a source of fascination, wonder, and perplexity for millennia. They are a nightly voyage into the uncharted territories of our subconscious, a realm where logic and reason often take a back seat to symbolism and metaphor. As we navigate this surreal landscape, we encounter a multitude of images, emotions, and sensations that can leave us feeling both bewildered and intrigued upon waking. But what do these nocturnal adventures mean? How can we decipher the hidden messages that our dreams are trying to convey?

The Dreamer's Handbook is your guide to unraveling the mysteries of your dreams. It's a comprehensive guide that will equip you with the tools and knowledge you need to interpret your dreams and unlock their hidden wisdom. Whether you're a seasoned dreamer or a novice explorer of the dream world, this handbook will provide you with valuable insights into the language of dreams, the symbolism of common dream themes, and the various techniques you can use to decode your own unique dream language.

First and foremost, it's important to understand that dream interpretation is a deeply personal and subjective process. There is no one-size-fits-all approach to deciphering the meaning of your dreams. The same symbol can have different meanings for different people, depending on their individual experiences, cultural background, and emotional state. Therefore, the first step in interpreting your dreams is to cultivate a deep understanding of your own unique dream language.

To begin this journey of self-discovery, start by keeping a dream journal. A dream journal is a powerful tool that allows you to capture the fleeting images and emotions of your dreams before they fade from memory. By recording your dreams on a regular basis, you can begin to identify patterns, recurring themes, and personal symbols that shed light on your inner world.

As you record your dreams, pay attention to the details. What were the people, places, and objects that appeared in your dream? How did they interact with each other and with you? What emotions did you experience during the dream? Were you happy, sad, scared, or angry? These details and emotions can provide important clues about the underlying meaning of your dream.

Once you have recorded your dream, take some time to reflect on it. Ask yourself what the dream might be trying to tell you. What are the possible meanings of the symbols and themes that appeared in your dream? How does the dream relate to your waking life? What emotions did the dream evoke, and what might those emotions be telling you?

To help you with this process, The Dreamer's Handbook provides a comprehensive overview of common dream symbols and their potential meanings. For example, water often represents our emotions and the unconscious mind, while flying can symbolize freedom, ambition, or spiritual transcendence. Falling may indicate insecurity, vulnerability, or a fear of failure, while being chased can reflect feelings of anxiety, guilt, or unresolved conflict.

However, it's important to remember that these are just general interpretations. The true meaning of a symbol in your dream will depend on your personal associations and the context of the dream. For example, a snake may represent danger and temptation for one person, while it may symbolize healing and transformation for another.

In addition to exploring the symbolism of your dreams, The Dreamer's Handbook also provides a variety of techniques for interpreting your dreams. These techniques include free association, active imagination, and dream re-entry. Free association involves allowing your mind to wander freely as you think about your dream, while active imagination involves consciously interacting with the characters and symbols in your dream. Dream re-entry involves returning to your dream in a relaxed state and exploring it further.

Another valuable tool for interpreting your dreams is dream incubation. This technique involves setting an intention before bed to dream about a specific topic or issue. By focusing your mind on a particular question or problem before you sleep, you can increase the likelihood of receiving guidance or insights in your dreams.

As you delve deeper into the world of dreams, you may discover that your dreams are not just random firings of neurons, but rather a profound source of wisdom, creativity, and self-discovery. By learning to interpret your dreams, you can gain a deeper understanding of yourself, your relationships, and your place in the world. You can also tap into your intuition, confront your fears, and unlock your hidden potential.

The Dreamer's Handbook is your companion on this journey of self-discovery. It's a comprehensive guide that will equip you with the tools and knowledge you need to interpret your dreams and unlock their hidden wisdom. By following the guidance in this handbook, you can begin to unravel the mysteries of your dreams and awaken to a life of greater meaning, purpose, and fulfillment.

ϷϷϷ

The Dream Therapist is a skilled navigator of the dream world, helping you decipher its cryptic messages and navigate its treacherous terrain. Trust their expertise, and together you can unlock the healing power of your dreams.

SEVEN

NIGHTLY ADVENTURES: EXPLORING THE WORLD OF YOUR DREAMS.

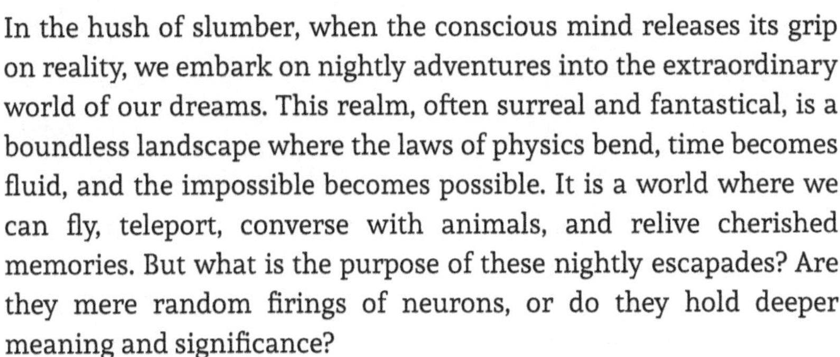

In the hush of slumber, when the conscious mind releases its grip on reality, we embark on nightly adventures into the extraordinary world of our dreams. This realm, often surreal and fantastical, is a boundless landscape where the laws of physics bend, time becomes fluid, and the impossible becomes possible. It is a world where we can fly, teleport, converse with animals, and relive cherished memories. But what is the purpose of these nightly escapades? Are they mere random firings of neurons, or do they hold deeper meaning and significance?

Dreams have fascinated and perplexed humanity for millennia. They have been interpreted as omens, prophecies, and messages from the divine. Ancient civilizations, such as the Egyptians and

Greeks, believed that dreams were a direct line of communication with the gods. They built elaborate dream temples and consulted dream interpreters to decipher the hidden meanings within their nightly visions.

Modern science has offered a more rational understanding of dreams, but their significance and potential for self-discovery remain undeniable. Dreams are a reflection of our subconscious mind, a vast reservoir of thoughts, feelings, and experiences that lie beneath the surface of our conscious awareness. This hidden realm is constantly processing information, sorting through memories, and making connections that our waking minds may not perceive. Dreams provide a unique opportunity to tap into this vast storehouse of knowledge and gain a deeper understanding of ourselves.

One of the most captivating aspects of dreams is their ability to transport us to unfamiliar and fantastical worlds. We may find ourselves soaring through the air, exploring underwater cities, or venturing into outer space. These otherworldly landscapes often mirror our own internal states, reflecting our emotions, desires, and fears. For example, a dream of flying may symbolize a sense of freedom and liberation, while a dream of drowning may represent feelings of overwhelm or helplessness.

Dreams can also transport us back in time, allowing us to relive cherished memories or revisit unresolved conflicts. We may encounter loved ones who have passed away, or we may find ourselves back in childhood, facing challenges that we thought we had long overcome. These dream experiences can offer valuable insights into our past, helping us to make sense of our present and chart a course for our future.

Another intriguing aspect of dreams is their ability to defy the laws of logic and reason. We may encounter talking animals, impossible scenarios, and bizarre transformations. These dream anomalies often serve as metaphors for the complexities and contradictions of our own lives. For example, a dream of a talking animal may represent a hidden aspect of our personality or a message from our intuition.

Dreams can also be a source of creativity and inspiration. Many artists, writers, and musicians have credited their dreams with sparking their creative genius. For example, Paul McCartney reportedly composed the melody for the Beatles' hit song "Yesterday" in a dream. Mary Shelley's "Frankenstein" was also inspired by a vivid nightmare.

The world of dreams is a vast and ever-changing landscape, full of surprises and hidden treasures. By exploring this realm with curiosity and openness, we can gain valuable insights into our innermost selves and our place in the universe. Dream exploration is a journey of self-discovery, a way to connect with our subconscious mind and tap into our hidden potential.

There are many ways to explore the world of your dreams. One simple but effective method is to keep a dream journal. By recording your dreams as soon as you wake up, you can capture the details and emotions before they fade from memory. Over time, patterns and recurring themes may emerge, revealing valuable insights into your subconscious mind.

Another way to explore your dreams is to practice lucid dreaming. Lucid dreaming is the ability to become aware that you are dreaming while you are still asleep. This awareness allows you to consciously influence the dream narrative, creating your own dream adventures and exploring your innermost desires.

Whether you choose to explore your dreams through journaling, lucid dreaming, or simply paying closer attention to their details and emotions, the rewards can be immense. Dreams can offer guidance, inspiration, and a deeper understanding of yourself and your place in the world. So embrace your nightly adventures and discover the hidden treasures that await you in the world of your dreams.

ϼϼϼ

Embrace the art of dreaming, and watch as your nights become a canvas for creative expression and emotional exploration. Allow your imagination to run wild, and you may be surprised by the insights and inspirations that arise.

EIGHT

THE DREAM WEAVER'S TOOLKIT: TOOLS FOR UNDERSTANDING YOUR DREAMS.

Dreams, those enigmatic tapestries woven in the loom of our sleeping minds, have been a source of fascination, wonder, and perplexity for millennia. They are a nightly voyage into the uncharted territories of our subconscious, a realm where logic and reason often take a back seat to symbolism and metaphor. To navigate this surreal landscape and decipher the hidden messages that our dreams are trying to convey, we need a set of tools – a Dream Weaver's Toolkit.

The first and most essential tool in this toolkit is a dream journal. Much like a cartographer mapping uncharted lands, a dream journal allows us to chart the course of our nocturnal journeys. Upon waking, jot down as many details as you can recall – the characters, settings, emotions, and any recurring symbols. This practice not only strengthens your dream recall but also reveals patterns and themes over time, offering valuable insights into your subconscious mind.

Accompanying the dream journal is the pen, a seemingly simple yet indispensable instrument. The act of writing engages both the logical and creative aspects of our brain, facilitating a deeper connection with our dreams. As you transcribe your dream, pay attention to the words that flow effortlessly onto the page. These words may hold clues to the underlying meaning of your dream, revealing hidden emotions or unspoken desires.

Another valuable tool in the Dream Weaver's Toolkit is a dream dictionary. This reference book provides interpretations of common dream symbols, offering a starting point for understanding your own unique dream language. While dream dictionaries can be helpful, it's important to remember that they are not definitive. The meaning of a symbol can vary depending on the individual's personal experiences, cultural background, and emotional state. Therefore, use the dream dictionary as a springboard for your own exploration, allowing your intuition to guide you towards the most meaningful interpretation.

In addition to these physical tools, there are also several mental and emotional techniques that can enhance your dream understanding. One such technique is dream incubation. Before you drift off to sleep, set an intention to dream about a specific topic or issue. This can be as simple as asking a question or visualizing a particular scenario. By focusing your mind on a specific intention, you increase the likelihood of receiving guidance or insights in your dreams.

Another powerful technique is lucid dreaming. Lucid dreaming is the ability to become aware that you are dreaming while you are still asleep. This awareness allows you to consciously participate in and even direct the dream narrative. Lucid dreaming can be a transformative experience, providing a unique opportunity for self-exploration, problem-solving, and creative expression.

To cultivate lucid dreaming, there are several practices you can incorporate into your daily routine. Reality checks, where you periodically question whether you are awake or dreaming, can help you become more aware of your state of consciousness. Dream journaling and maintaining a consistent sleep schedule can also promote lucid dreaming.

Meditation and mindfulness practices can also enhance your dream recall and understanding. By quieting the mind and focusing on the present moment, you create a space for your subconscious to communicate with you through your dreams. Regular meditation can also help you to become more aware of your thoughts and emotions, both in waking life and in dreams.

Engaging with creative outlets, such as art, music, or writing, can also deepen your connection with your dreams. Dreams are often rich in imagery and symbolism, and expressing these elements through creative mediums can unlock hidden meanings and insights. For example, painting a dream scene can help you to visualize and process the emotions associated with the dream, while writing a dream poem can capture its essence and distill its message.

The Dream Weaver's Toolkit is a dynamic and ever-evolving collection of tools and techniques. As you continue to explore the world of your dreams, you may discover new methods and resources that resonate with you. The key is to remain open to experimentation and to trust your intuition. Remember, dream interpretation is a personal journey, and the tools that work best for you may not be the same as those that work for others.

By embracing the Dream Weaver's Toolkit, you empower yourself to unravel the mysteries of your dreams and unlock their hidden wisdom. Whether you seek guidance, inspiration, or a deeper understanding of yourself, your dreams are a rich source of knowledge and insight. So gather your tools, trust your intuition, and embark on a nightly adventure into the boundless realm of your dreams.

ϷϷϷ

Just as an alchemist transforms base metals into gold, you can transform your dreams into wisdom through the art of dream alchemy. Explore the symbolism, emotions, and themes of your dreams, and uncover the hidden truths they reveal.

NINE

BEYOND REALITY: JOURNEYING THROUGH THE LANDSCAPE OF YOUR DREAMS.

In the hush of slumber, when the world retreats and our conscious minds release their grip on reality, we embark on a wondrous journey – a journey beyond reality, into the vast and enigmatic landscape of our dreams. This nocturnal odyssey is a voyage of self-discovery, a pilgrimage to the innermost recesses of our being. It is a realm where the ordinary transforms into the extraordinary, where the mundane becomes symbolic, and where the impossible becomes possible.

As we traverse this dreamscape, we encounter a multitude of landscapes, each one a reflection of our inner world. We may find ourselves strolling through lush meadows, symbolizing our connection to nature and our desire for peace and tranquility. We may climb towering mountains, representing our ambition and our quest for self-improvement. We may wander through labyrinthine cities, reflecting the complexities and contradictions of our lives. Or we may find ourselves adrift on a vast ocean, symbolizing the depths of our unconscious mind and the vastness of the unknown.

These landscapes are not merely static backdrops, but living, breathing entities that interact with us and shape our dream experiences. They may offer us guidance, challenge us with obstacles, or provide a safe haven for our deepest fears and desires. By paying attention to the details of these landscapes, we can glean valuable insights into our subconscious mind and our waking lives.

The characters we encounter in our dreams are also integral to our journey through the dreamscape. These characters may be familiar faces from our waking lives, or they may be archetypal figures that represent universal aspects of human nature. We may encounter wise elders, mischievous tricksters, or fearsome monsters. Each character serves a purpose in our dream narrative, offering us challenges, lessons, or opportunities for growth.

The emotions we experience in our dreams are another crucial element of our nocturnal adventures. Dreams can evoke a wide range of emotions, from joy and excitement to fear and anger. These emotions are often amplified in the dream state, making them feel more intense and visceral. By paying attention to our dream emotions, we can gain valuable insights into our subconscious feelings and attitudes.

As we journey through the landscape of our dreams, we may encounter a variety of challenges and obstacles. We may be chased by monsters, trapped in labyrinthine mazes, or confronted with our deepest fears. These challenges often mirror the obstacles we face in our waking lives, and overcoming them in our dreams can empower us to overcome them in reality.

Dreams can also offer us glimpses of our hidden potential. We may find ourselves performing superhuman feats, solving complex problems, or creating works of art that surpass our waking abilities. These dream experiences can inspire us to reach for our goals and fulfill our potential in our waking lives.

In addition to the landscapes, characters, and emotions we encounter in our dreams, there are also a variety of dream phenomena that can enrich our nocturnal adventures. Lucid dreaming, for example, is the ability to become aware that we are dreaming while we are still asleep. This awareness allows us to consciously participate in and even direct the dream narrative, creating our own dream adventures and exploring our innermost desires.

Another fascinating dream phenomenon is precognitive dreaming, where we dream of events that later come to pass in our waking lives. While the scientific evidence for precognitive dreaming is inconclusive, many people report having experienced such dreams. Whether or not precognitive dreams are real, they offer a tantalizing glimpse into the possibility that our dreams may be connected to a deeper reality beyond our waking consciousness.

As we journey through the landscape of our dreams, we embark on a voyage of self-discovery, a pilgrimage to the innermost recesses of our being. By paying attention to the details of our dreams, exploring their symbolism, and embracing their emotional intensity, we can unlock a wealth of wisdom, creativity, and personal growth. So let us embrace our nightly adventures and discover the hidden treasures that await us in the boundless realm of our dreams.

ᖘᖘᖘ

Lucid dreaming is a magical experience, a state of heightened awareness where you can consciously participate in and even direct your dreams. Embrace this power, and watch as your dreams become a playground for self-discovery and personal growth.

TEN

THE DREAMER'S JOURNAL: A GUIDE TO RECORDING AND INTERPRETING YOUR DREAMS.

As the sun dips below the horizon, casting long shadows and painting the sky in hues of orange and purple, our bodies prepare for slumber. But as our physical forms rest, our minds embark on a different kind of journey – a journey into the vast and enigmatic landscape of our dreams. In this ethereal realm, we encounter a multitude of images, emotions, and experiences that often leave us feeling bewildered and intrigued upon waking. But what do these nightly visions mean? How can we decipher the hidden messages that our dreams are trying to convey?

One of the most powerful tools for unlocking the mysteries of our dreams is the Dreamer's Journal. This simple yet profound practice involves recording our dreams upon waking, capturing the fleeting images and emotions before they fade from memory. As we document our dreams, we begin to notice patterns, recurring themes, and personal symbols that shed light on our subconscious mind and our waking lives.

The Dreamer's Journal serves as a bridge between our conscious and subconscious minds. It provides a space for us to reflect on our dreams, to explore their meanings, and to integrate their messages into our daily lives. By engaging with our dreams in this way, we can tap into their wisdom, creativity, and healing potential.

To begin your journey with the Dreamer's Journal, simply find a notebook and pen that you feel drawn to. It's helpful to keep the journal by your bedside so that you can easily reach for it upon waking. As soon as you awaken from a dream, take a few moments to center yourself and recall the details of the dream. Write down as much as you can remember, including the characters, settings, emotions, and any symbols or themes that stand out. Don't worry about grammar or spelling – the most important thing is to capture the essence of the dream.

As you record your dreams, be as descriptive as possible. Use vivid language to paint a picture of the dream world and the emotions you experienced. Include sensory details, such as sights, sounds, smells, tastes, and touch. The more detailed your description, the easier it will be to recall and interpret the dream later on.

Once you have recorded the dream, take some time to reflect on it. Ask yourself what the dream might be trying to tell you. What are the possible meanings of the symbols and themes that appeared in the dream? How does the dream relate to your waking life? What emotions did the dream evoke, and what might those emotions be telling you?

To help you with this process, you can refer to dream dictionaries and other resources on dream interpretation. However, it's important to remember that these resources should be used as a starting point for your own personal exploration. The most meaningful interpretations will come from your own intuition and understanding of your unique dream language.

As you continue to journal your dreams, you may begin to notice recurring symbols, themes, and patterns. These can provide valuable insights into your subconscious mind and your waking life. For example, recurring dreams of flying may indicate a desire for freedom or a need to break free from limitations. Recurring dreams of water may symbolize emotional turmoil or a need for emotional cleansing.

By paying attention to these recurring patterns, you can begin to identify the underlying issues that your dreams are trying to address. You may discover hidden fears, anxieties, or unresolved conflicts that are influencing your waking life. By bringing these issues to light, you can begin to address them and move towards healing and wholeness.

Dream journaling can also help you to tap into your creativity and intuition. Dreams often contain vivid imagery and symbolic language that can spark creative inspiration. By paying attention to these creative elements, you can tap into your own artistic potential and use it to express yourself in new and meaningful ways.

In addition to recording and interpreting your dreams, the Dreamer's Journal can also be used to track your sleep patterns, identify any potential sleep disorders, and monitor your overall well-being. By tracking your sleep quality, you can identify any factors that may be affecting your sleep, such as stress, caffeine, or alcohol.

The Dreamer's Journal is a powerful tool for self-discovery, healing, and personal growth. By engaging with our dreams in a meaningful way, we can unlock their hidden wisdom and potential. Whether you are seeking guidance, inspiration, or a deeper understanding of yourself, the Dreamer's Journal can help you to navigate the mysterious and magical world of your dreams.

ᗡᗡᗡ

Your dream journal is a treasure trove of insights, a chronicle of your subconscious mind's wanderings. Review it regularly, and you may discover recurring patterns and symbols that offer valuable guidance on your life's journey.

ELEVEN

WHISPERS OF THE NIGHT: DECIPHERING THE LANGUAGE OF DREAMS.

In the hushed stillness of the night, as we surrender to slumber's embrace, our minds embark on extraordinary journeys through a realm where reality bends and imagination reigns supreme. This is the world of dreams, a landscape rich with symbolism, emotion, and hidden messages. To truly understand ourselves and our place in the universe, we must learn to decipher the whispers of the night, to interpret the language of dreams.

Throughout history, dreams have captivated and mystified humanity. Ancient civilizations revered dreams as messages from the gods, while modern psychologists view them as a window into the subconscious mind. Regardless of their origin or purpose, dreams hold a wealth of information about our inner selves. They can reveal our deepest fears and desires, offer guidance on our life path, and even spark creative inspiration.

The language of dreams is often symbolic and metaphorical, requiring a different mode of interpretation than our waking language. Dreams speak to us through images, emotions, and sensations, rather than words. To decipher this language, we must learn to listen with our hearts and minds, to pay attention to the subtle nuances of our dreams, and to trust our intuition.

One of the most common ways that dreams communicate with us is through recurring symbols. These symbols may appear in different forms and contexts, but they often carry a consistent message. Water, for example, is a universal symbol that can represent our emotions, the unconscious mind, or the flow of life. Dreaming of calm water may symbolize peace and tranquility, while turbulent water may indicate emotional turmoil or unresolved conflicts.

Animals are also frequent visitors in our dreams, often symbolizing different aspects of our own personalities or instincts. A snake, for example, may represent hidden knowledge or transformation, while a lion may symbolize courage and leadership. The type of animal and its behavior in the dream can provide important clues to its meaning.

Dreams can also speak to us through emotions. The emotions we experience in our dreams often reflect our underlying feelings about the events and situations depicted in the dream. For example, a dream about a loved one may evoke feelings of happiness and nostalgia, while a dream about a traumatic event may trigger feelings of fear and anxiety.

By paying attention to the symbols and emotions that appear in our dreams, we can begin to uncover their hidden messages. We may discover recurring themes that reflect our core values, beliefs, and aspirations. We may also gain insights into our relationships, career choices, and personal struggles.

There are many techniques for deciphering the language of dreams. One of the most effective is dream journaling. By recording our dreams as soon as we wake up, we can capture the details and emotions before they fade from memory. Over time, patterns and recurring themes may emerge, revealing valuable insights into our subconscious mind.

Another helpful technique is to share our dreams with others. Talking to a trusted friend, therapist, or dream interpreter can help us to make sense of our dreams and uncover their hidden meanings.

Dream dictionaries can also be a useful resource for interpreting common dream symbols. However, it's important to remember that these dictionaries are not definitive, and the meaning of a symbol can vary depending on the individual's personal associations and experiences.

Ultimately, the most effective way to decipher the language of dreams is to approach them with curiosity, openness, and a willingness to explore the depths of our own psyche. By paying attention to the symbols, emotions, and themes that appear in our dreams, we can gain valuable insights into our innermost selves and our journey through life.

Dreams are a gift from our subconscious, offering us a glimpse into the hidden workings of our minds. By learning to decipher their messages, we can awaken to a deeper understanding of ourselves and our place in the universe. So let us embrace the whispers of the night and embark on a journey of self-discovery through the language of dreams.

ᗐᗐᗐ

Dreams are not just for sleep; they are a bridge between the conscious and subconscious minds. By understanding the language of dreams, you can build a stronger connection with your inner self and unlock your full potential.

TWELVE

FROM SLUMBER TO INSIGHT: DISCOVERING THE MEANING OF YOUR DREAMS.

In the realm of dreams, the boundaries between the conscious and subconscious blur, offering us a unique opportunity to delve into the depths of our inner selves. As we surrender to slumber's embrace, our minds embark on extraordinary journeys, traversing landscapes both familiar and fantastical, encountering characters both beloved and enigmatic. Within these nocturnal narratives lie hidden messages, whispers of insight waiting to be deciphered. The journey from slumber to insight begins with recognizing that dreams are not mere fleeting illusions, but rather a profound language through which our subconscious communicates with us.

The first step in this journey is to cultivate a sense of curiosity and openness towards our dreams. Rather than dismissing them as random neural firings, we must embrace them as a potential source of wisdom and guidance. By approaching our dreams with a receptive attitude, we create a space for their messages to emerge.

Keeping a dream journal is a powerful tool for capturing and preserving the ephemeral nature of dreams. As soon as you awaken, jot down as many details as you can recall, no matter how trivial or bizarre they may seem. Describe the characters, settings, emotions, and any symbols or recurring themes that stand out. This practice not only strengthens your dream recall but also reveals patterns and connections that may not be immediately apparent.

As you review your dream journal, pay attention to the emotions that your dreams evoke. Were you filled with joy, fear, anger, or sadness? These emotions can provide valuable clues about the underlying meaning of your dream. For example, a recurring dream of being chased may indicate feelings of anxiety or unresolved conflict, while a dream of soaring through the air may symbolize a sense of freedom or liberation.

Next, consider the symbolism within your dreams. Dreams often communicate through metaphors, allegories, and archetypes. Common dream symbols, such as water, flying, falling, and being chased, can carry universal meanings that resonate with people across cultures and time periods. However, the interpretation of these symbols can also be highly personal, depending on your individual experiences and associations.

For example, water in a dream may represent emotions, the unconscious mind, or the flow of life. Dreaming of calm water may symbolize peace and tranquility, while turbulent water may indicate emotional turmoil or unresolved conflicts. Similarly, flying dreams often evoke feelings of freedom, liberation, and empowerment, while falling dreams may represent insecurity, vulnerability, or a fear of failure.

By exploring the symbolism within your dreams, you can begin to decipher their hidden messages. A dream of being trapped in a labyrinth, for example, may symbolize feeling lost or stuck in a particular situation. A dream of finding a hidden treasure may represent a discovery of your own inner strengths or talents.

In addition to exploring the symbolism and emotions within your dreams, it can be helpful to consider the context in which they occur. Are there any recurring themes or patterns that emerge over time? Do your dreams seem to be influenced by events or experiences in your waking life? By examining the context of your dreams, you can gain a deeper understanding of their meaning and relevance to your life.

Seeking guidance from others can also be a valuable step in the dream interpretation process. Sharing your dreams with a trusted friend, therapist, or dream interpreter can provide new perspectives and interpretations that you may not have considered on your own. They can also help you to identify any blind spots or biases in your own interpretations.

Ultimately, the most meaningful interpretations of your dreams will come from within. Trust your intuition and allow your dreams to speak to you in their own unique language. By cultivating a sense of curiosity, openness, and self-reflection, you can embark on a transformative journey from slumber to insight, discovering the hidden messages that your dreams hold for you.

ppp

In the depths of slumber, your subconscious whispers secrets that your waking mind may not be ready to hear. Listen carefully to these whispers, and you may discover hidden truths that can transform your life.

THIRTEEN

THE DREAM ORACLE: USING YOUR DREAMS FOR GUIDANCE AND INSIGHT.

In the tapestry of human experience, dreams have long been revered as a profound source of wisdom and guidance. Throughout history, cultures across the globe have sought to interpret the enigmatic messages woven into the fabric of our slumbering minds. From ancient oracles seeking divine prophecies to modern therapists exploring the depths of the subconscious, dreams have been seen as a portal to a realm beyond the waking world, a realm where hidden truths and profound insights await those who dare to venture within.

As the sun sets and the shadows lengthen, we surrender to the embrace of sleep, and our minds embark on extraordinary journeys through a landscape where the ordinary transforms into the extraordinary. We soar through the sky, converse with animals, relive cherished memories, and confront our deepest fears. These nocturnal adventures are not merely fleeting illusions, but rather a profound language through which our subconscious communicates with us.

The Dream Oracle invites us to embrace this language, to unlock the hidden meanings within our dreams and harness their transformative power. By delving into the depths of our nocturnal narratives, we can gain valuable insights into our deepest desires, fears, and unresolved conflicts. We can discover hidden talents, tap into our intuition, and find guidance on our life path.

At its core, the Dream Oracle is a tool for self-discovery and personal growth. It encourages us to view our dreams not as random neural firings, but as a reflection of our innermost selves. By paying attention to the symbols, emotions, and themes that appear in our dreams, we can gain a deeper understanding of our subconscious motivations and desires.

One of the most powerful ways to tap into the wisdom of the Dream Oracle is through dream journaling. By recording our dreams upon waking, we can capture their fleeting essence and begin to decipher their hidden messages. As we document our dreams, we may notice recurring patterns, symbols, and themes that offer valuable insights into our waking lives. For example, a recurring dream of being chased may indicate a fear of confrontation or a need to address unresolved conflicts, while a dream of flying may symbolize a desire for freedom or a sense of empowerment.

Another powerful tool for accessing the Dream Oracle is dream incubation. This technique involves setting an intention before bed to dream about a specific topic or issue. By focusing our minds on a particular question or problem before we sleep, we can increase the likelihood of receiving guidance or insights in our dreams. For example, if we are struggling with a decision, we can ask our dreams to provide us with clarity and direction.

As we explore the Dream Oracle, we may discover that our dreams offer us a glimpse into the future. Precognitive dreams, or dreams that seem to predict future events, have been reported throughout history. While the scientific evidence for precognitive dreams is inconclusive, many people believe that they have experienced such dreams. Whether or not precognitive dreams are real, they offer a tantalizing glimpse into the possibility that our dreams may be connected to a deeper reality beyond our waking consciousness.

The Dream Oracle is not just a tool for personal growth, but also a source of creative inspiration. Many artists, writers, and musicians have credited their dreams with sparking their creative genius. For example, Paul McCartney reportedly composed the melody for the Beatles' hit song "Yesterday" in a dream, while Mary Shelley's "Frankenstein" was inspired by a vivid nightmare.

By embracing the Dream Oracle, we open ourselves to a world of infinite possibilities. We learn to trust our intuition, confront our fears, and tap into our hidden potential. We discover that our dreams are not merely fleeting illusions, but a profound language that speaks to the very core of our being. By learning to listen to this language, we can awaken to a deeper understanding of ourselves and our place in the universe.

The Dream Oracle invites us to embark on a journey of self-discovery, to explore the hidden landscapes of our minds, and to embrace the transformative power of our dreams. As we delve into the depths of our nocturnal narratives, we may find that the answers we seek have been within us all along, waiting to be revealed in the whispers of the night.

ᘉᘉᘉ

The dream world is a place of infinite possibilities, where anything can happen. Embrace the unexpected, and you may find that your dreams lead you to places you never imagined possible.

FOURTEEN

DREAMSCAPE: NAVIGATING THE WORLD OF YOUR DREAMS.

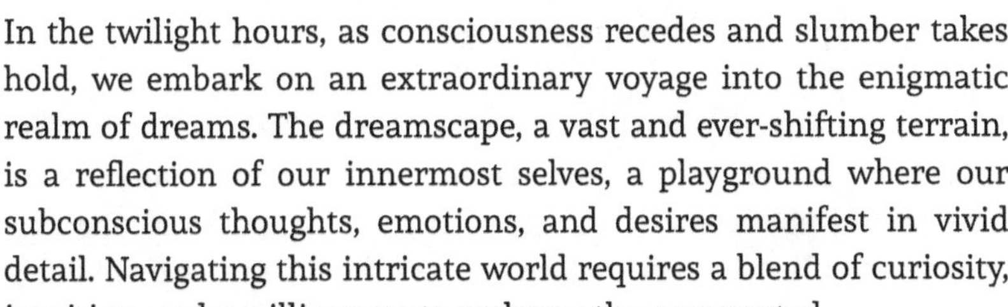

In the twilight hours, as consciousness recedes and slumber takes hold, we embark on an extraordinary voyage into the enigmatic realm of dreams. The dreamscape, a vast and ever-shifting terrain, is a reflection of our innermost selves, a playground where our subconscious thoughts, emotions, and desires manifest in vivid detail. Navigating this intricate world requires a blend of curiosity, intuition, and a willingness to embrace the unexpected.

The dreamscape is a realm of boundless possibilities, where the laws of physics and logic often give way to the whims of our imagination. We may find ourselves soaring through the air, exploring underwater cities, or conversing with fantastical creatures.

The settings of our dreams can be familiar and comforting, such as our childhood homes or favorite vacation spots, or they can be entirely unfamiliar and disorienting, transporting us to alien landscapes or surreal dimensions.

These dream settings are not merely static backdrops, but rather active participants in our dream narratives. They can evoke powerful emotions, trigger memories, and symbolize aspects of our waking lives.

For example, a dream of being lost in a forest may represent feelings of confusion or uncertainty, while a dream of standing on a mountaintop may symbolize a sense of accomplishment or clarity.

The characters we encounter in our dreams are equally significant. They may be familiar faces from our waking lives, such as family members, friends, or colleagues. Or they may be archetypal figures, such as the wise old man, the trickster, or the shadow self.

These dream characters often represent different aspects of our own personalities, or they may symbolize people or situations that we are grappling with in our waking lives.

The interactions we have with these dream characters can offer valuable insights into our relationships and interpersonal dynamics. For example, a dream of arguing with a loved one may reflect a conflict that needs to be addressed, while a dream of being embraced by a stranger may symbolize a need for connection and support.

As we navigate the dreamscape, we may also encounter a variety of dream symbols. These symbols can be objects, animals, or even abstract concepts. They often carry personal and universal meanings that can shed light on our subconscious thoughts and feelings. For example, a dream of a snake may represent transformation or healing, while a dream of a ladder may symbolize progress or ambition.

Interpreting dream symbols requires a combination of intuition, personal reflection, and cultural knowledge. It is important to consider the context of the dream, as well as your own personal associations with the symbols involved. For example, a dream of a spider may evoke fear in one person, while it may represent creativity and resourcefulness in another.

Emotions play a crucial role in our dream experiences. Dreams can evoke a wide range of emotions, from joy and excitement to fear and anger. These emotions can be triggered by the events and characters in our dreams, or they may simply arise from the depths of our subconscious.

Paying attention to our dream emotions can help us to identify and process unresolved feelings in our waking lives.

In addition to the landscapes, characters, symbols, and emotions we encounter in our dreams, there are also a variety of dream phenomena that can enrich our nocturnal adventures. Lucid dreaming, for example, is the ability to become aware that we are dreaming while we are still asleep.

This awareness allows us to consciously participate in and even direct the dream narrative, creating our own dream adventures and exploring our innermost desires.

Another fascinating dream phenomenon is precognitive dreaming, where we dream of events that later come to pass in our waking lives. While the scientific evidence for precognitive dreaming is inconclusive, many people report having experienced such dreams.

Whether or not precognitive dreams are real, they offer a tantalizing glimpse into the possibility that our dreams may be connected to a deeper reality beyond our waking consciousness.

As we navigate the world of our dreams, we embark on a journey of self-discovery, a pilgrimage to the innermost recesses of our being. By paying attention to the details of our dreams, exploring their symbolism, and embracing their emotional intensity, we can unlock a wealth of wisdom, creativity, and personal growth. So let us embrace our nightly adventures and discover the hidden treasures that await us in the boundless realm of our dreams.

ᗡᗡᗡ

Your dreams are a reflection of your deepest desires, fears, and anxieties. By confronting these emotions in the dream world, you can gain the courage to face them in your waking life.

FIFTEEN

THE POWER OF DREAMS: UNLOCKING THE POTENTIAL OF YOUR DREAMS.

the quiet hours of the night, when the world around us rests and our conscious minds recede, our dreams emerge from the depths of our subconscious, offering a glimpse into a realm of limitless possibilities. Dreams, often shrouded in mystery and symbolism, hold a profound power within them—a power that can inspire, heal, and guide us on our journey through life.

The human fascination with dreams spans cultures and centuries. Ancient civilizations revered dreams as messages from the divine, while modern science seeks to understand their neurological origins. Whether viewed as mystical or biological, one thing remains clear: dreams possess an undeniable power to unlock the potential of our minds and souls.

At their core, dreams are a reflection of our innermost selves. They mirror our deepest desires, fears, and unresolved conflicts. By paying close attention to the intricate tapestry of our dreams, we can gain valuable insights into our subconscious thoughts and emotions.

We may discover hidden talents, unresolved traumas, or untapped sources of creativity.

Dreams can serve as a powerful tool for personal growth and self-discovery. They can illuminate our blind spots, challenge our assumptions, and encourage us to step outside our comfort zones. For instance, a recurring dream of public speaking may reveal a hidden fear of judgment or a desire to express oneself more confidently. By confronting this fear in the dream world, we may find the courage to face it in our waking lives.

Moreover, dreams can offer us solutions to problems that have been eluding us in our waking state. The subconscious mind, unburdened by the constraints of logic and reason, can often make connections and generate ideas that our conscious mind cannot.

By incubating a problem before bed and paying attention to our dreams, we may receive unexpected insights or solutions that lead to breakthroughs in our personal or professional lives.

The power of dreams extends beyond personal growth and problem-solving. They can also serve as a source of creative inspiration. Many artists, writers, and musicians have credited their dreams with sparking their creative genius.

For example, the surrealist painter Salvador Dali drew inspiration from his bizarre and often disturbing dreams, while the musician Paul McCartney famously composed the melody for the Beatles' hit song "Yesterday" in a dream.

Dreams can also be a source of comfort and healing. They can provide a safe space to process difficult emotions, confront past traumas, and explore our deepest fears. For example, a person who has experienced a traumatic event may have recurring nightmares about the event. By working with a therapist or dream expert to understand and process these dreams, they may be able to find healing and closure.

Unlocking the potential of our dreams requires a willingness to engage with them actively. This means paying attention to the details of our dreams, exploring their symbolism, and reflecting on their emotional impact.

Keeping a dream journal is a powerful tool for capturing and analyzing our dreams. By recording our dreams upon waking, we can create a record of our nocturnal journeys and uncover patterns and themes that may not be immediately apparent.

In addition to journaling, there are many other techniques for unlocking the potential of our dreams. Dream incubation, as mentioned earlier, involves setting an intention before bed to dream about a specific topic or issue. Lucid dreaming, the ability to become aware that you are dreaming while you are still asleep, can also be a powerful tool for self-exploration and creativity.

Ultimately, the power of dreams lies in their ability to connect us with our deepest selves. By embracing our dreams as a valuable source of wisdom, guidance, and inspiration, we open ourselves to a world of infinite possibilities.

We may discover hidden talents, overcome our fears, find creative solutions to problems, and ultimately, live more fulfilling and meaningful lives.

The journey into the world of dreams is a personal and transformative one. It requires courage, curiosity, and a willingness to embrace the unknown. But the rewards are immeasurable. By unlocking the potential of our dreams, we unlock the potential of ourselves.

❦❦❦

Dreams are a source of creative inspiration, a wellspring of ideas and insights. Pay attention to the images and symbols that appear in your dreams, and you may find that they spark your next great work of art.

SIXTEEN

DREAM ALCHEMY: TRANSFORMING YOUR DREAMS INTO WISDOM.

In the quiet depths of slumber, our minds embark on extraordinary journeys, traversing landscapes both familiar and fantastical, encountering characters both beloved and enigmatic. These nocturnal odysseys, known as dreams, are not mere fleeting illusions but rather a profound language through which our subconscious communicates with us. Like alchemists of old, we can transform these raw materials of our dreams into wisdom, illuminating our waking lives and guiding us towards greater self-awareness and personal growth.

Throughout history, dreams have been revered as a source of divine inspiration, prophetic insight, and psychological understanding. Ancient civilizations, such as the Egyptians and Greeks, believed that dreams were messages from the gods, while modern psychologists view them as a window into the subconscious mind. Regardless of their origin or purpose, dreams hold a wealth of information about our innermost selves, offering a glimpse into our deepest desires, fears, and unresolved conflicts.

Dream alchemy is the art of transforming these raw materials of our dreams into wisdom. It involves actively engaging with our dreams, exploring their symbolism, and integrating their messages into our waking lives. By doing so, we can unlock the hidden potential within our dreams and use them as a catalyst for personal transformation.

The first step in dream alchemy is to cultivate a sense of curiosity and openness towards our dreams. Rather than dismissing them as random neural firings, we must embrace them as a potential source of wisdom and guidance. This involves paying attention to our dreams, recording them in a journal, and reflecting on their meaning and significance.

As we delve deeper into our dreams, we begin to notice recurring symbols, themes, and patterns. These recurring elements are not mere coincidences, but rather messages from our subconscious mind. By paying attention to these messages, we can gain valuable insights into our waking lives.

For example, recurring dreams of water may symbolize our emotions and the unconscious mind. Dreaming of calm water may indicate peace and tranquility, while turbulent water may suggest emotional turmoil or unresolved conflicts. Similarly, recurring dreams of flying may represent a desire for freedom or liberation, while recurring dreams of falling may indicate insecurity or a fear of failure.

By exploring the symbolism within our dreams, we can begin to decipher their hidden messages. We may discover recurring themes that reflect our core values, beliefs, and aspirations. We may also gain insights into our relationships, career choices, and personal struggles.

One of the most powerful tools for dream alchemy is dream incubation. This technique involves setting an intention before bed to dream about a specific topic or issue. By focusing our minds on a particular question or problem before we sleep, we can increase the likelihood of receiving guidance or insights in our dreams. For example, if we are struggling with a decision, we can ask our dreams to provide us with clarity and direction.

Another powerful tool for dream alchemy is lucid dreaming. Lucid dreaming is the ability to become aware that you are dreaming while you are still asleep. This awareness allows you to consciously participate in and even direct the dream narrative. Lucid dreaming can be a transformative experience, providing a unique opportunity for self-exploration, problem-solving, and creative expression.

As we continue to explore the world of our dreams, we may discover that they are not just a reflection of our inner selves, but also a source of inspiration and guidance. Dreams can offer us creative solutions to problems, help us to heal from past traumas, and guide us towards our true purpose in life.

By embracing the practice of dream alchemy, we open ourselves to a world of infinite possibilities. We learn to trust our intuition, confront our fears, and tap into our hidden potential. We discover that our dreams are not merely fleeting illusions, but a profound language that speaks to the very core of our being. By learning to listen to this language, we can awaken to a deeper understanding of ourselves and our place in the universe.

ppp

Your dreams are a safe space to explore your deepest fears and anxieties. By confronting these emotions in the dream world, you can learn to overcome them and live a more fulfilling life.

SEVENTEEN

THE DREAMER'S COMPASS: USING YOUR DREAMS TO FIND YOUR WAY.

In the vast landscape of our lives, we often find ourselves navigating through uncharted territories, facing crossroads and uncertainties. The path ahead may seem obscured, leaving us feeling lost and unsure of our direction. Yet, within the depths of our slumbering minds lies a powerful tool that can guide us through these murky waters – the Dreamer's Compass.

Dreams, those enigmatic tapestries woven in the loom of our subconscious, offer a unique perspective on our waking lives. They are a reflection of our innermost selves, a mirror that reveals our deepest desires, fears, and unresolved conflicts. By paying attention to the subtle whispers of our dreams, we can gain valuable insights that can help us navigate the challenges and opportunities that life presents us with.

The Dreamer's Compass is a metaphor for the guidance that our dreams can provide. Like a compass needle pointing towards true north, our dreams can guide us towards our true purpose, our passions, and our authentic selves. By learning to interpret the symbols, emotions, and themes that appear in our dreams, we can uncover hidden truths about ourselves and our lives.

One of the most common ways that dreams offer guidance is through recurring symbols. These symbols may appear in different forms and contexts, but they often carry a consistent message. For example, a recurring dream of water may symbolize our emotions, with calm water representing peace and tranquility, while turbulent water may indicate emotional turmoil or unresolved conflicts. Similarly, recurring dreams of flying may represent a desire for freedom or liberation, while recurring dreams of falling may indicate insecurity or a fear of failure.

By paying attention to these recurring symbols, we can begin to identify the underlying issues that our dreams are trying to address. We may discover hidden fears, anxieties, or unresolved conflicts that are influencing our waking lives. By bringing these issues to light, we can begin to address them and move towards healing and wholeness.

Dreams can also offer guidance through specific scenarios or situations. For example, a dream of being lost in a forest may indicate a feeling of confusion or uncertainty in our waking lives. By exploring the details of the dream, such as the emotions we experienced, the obstacles we encountered, and the actions we took, we can gain valuable insights into how to navigate similar situations in our waking lives.

Another way that dreams can guide us is through emotional experiences. The emotions we feel in our dreams often reflect our underlying feelings about the events and situations depicted in the dream. For example, a dream about a loved one may evoke feelings of happiness and nostalgia, while a dream about a traumatic event may trigger feelings of fear and anxiety. By paying attention to these emotions, we can gain a deeper understanding of our subconscious feelings and attitudes.

Dream journaling is a powerful tool for tapping into the wisdom of our dreams. By recording our dreams as soon as we wake up, we can capture the details and emotions before they fade from memory. Over time, patterns and recurring themes may emerge, revealing valuable insights into our subconscious mind.

Sharing our dreams with others can also be a helpful way to gain new perspectives and insights. Talking to a trusted friend, therapist, or dream interpreter can help us to make sense of our dreams and uncover their hidden meanings.

Ultimately, the Dreamer's Compass is a personal tool that requires both intuition and self-reflection. There is no one-size-fits-all approach to dream interpretation, and the meaning of a dream can vary depending on the individual's personal experiences and associations. However, by cultivating a sense of curiosity, openness, and a willingness to explore the depths of our own psyche, we can tap into the wisdom of our dreams and use it to find our way in life.

The Dreamer's Compass is a powerful tool for navigating the challenges and uncertainties of life. By paying attention to the messages of our dreams, we can gain valuable insights into our subconscious mind, our emotions, and our deepest desires. We can use this information to make better decisions, overcome obstacles, and live more fulfilling lives. So let us embrace the wisdom of our dreams and allow them to guide us on our journey through life.

ppp

The dream world is a realm of healing and transformation. By revisiting past traumas and exploring unresolved conflicts in your dreams, you can find closure and move forward on your healing journey.

EIGHTEEN

THE ART OF DREAMING: CULTIVATING A RICH DREAM LIFE.

Dreams are not merely fleeting illusions that vanish with the morning light; they are a vibrant tapestry woven into the fabric of our subconscious minds. Within their enigmatic landscapes lie hidden treasures of self-discovery, creativity, and healing. Embracing the art of dreaming allows us to unlock these treasures, to cultivate a rich and meaningful dream life that nourishes our waking existence.

The art of dreaming begins with an understanding that dreams are not random occurrences, but rather a reflection of our innermost selves. They are a language through which our subconscious communicates with us, offering insights into our deepest desires, fears, and unresolved conflicts. By paying attention to the symbols, emotions, and themes that appear in our dreams, we can gain a deeper understanding of ourselves and our place in the world.

Cultivating a rich dream life requires intention and dedication. It involves creating a sacred space for our dreams, both within our minds and in our physical environments. This can be as simple as setting aside a few minutes each day to reflect on our dreams, or as elaborate as creating a dream altar or sanctuary where we can connect with the dream world.

One of the most powerful tools for cultivating a rich dream life is dream journaling. By recording our dreams upon waking, we can capture their fleeting essence and begin to decipher their hidden messages. As we document our dreams, we may notice recurring patterns, symbols, and themes that offer valuable insights into our waking lives. Dream journaling also helps to strengthen our dream recall, making it easier to remember and interpret our dreams.

Another powerful tool for cultivating a rich dream life is dream incubation. This technique involves setting an intention before bed to dream about a specific topic or issue. By focusing our minds on a particular question or problem before we sleep, we can increase the likelihood of receiving guidance or insights in our dreams. Dream incubation can be used to explore personal challenges, seek creative solutions, or connect with spiritual guidance.

Lucid dreaming, the ability to become aware that you are dreaming while you are still asleep, is another valuable tool for cultivating a rich dream life. Lucid dreaming allows us to consciously participate in and even direct the dream narrative. This can be a transformative experience, providing a unique opportunity for self-exploration, problem-solving, and creative expression.

There are many techniques for inducing lucid dreams, such as reality checks, dream journaling, and meditation. By incorporating these practices into our daily routines, we can increase our chances of experiencing lucid dreams and unlocking their full potential.

In addition to these specific techniques, there are many other ways to cultivate a rich dream life. Engaging in creative activities, such as writing, painting, or music, can stimulate our imagination and enhance our dream recall. Spending time in nature can also connect us with the rhythms of the earth and the cycles of the moon, which can influence our dream patterns.

Paying attention to our diet and sleep hygiene is also crucial for cultivating a rich dream life. Eating a healthy diet, avoiding caffeine and alcohol before bed, and establishing a consistent sleep schedule can all contribute to better sleep quality and more vivid dreams.

As we cultivate a rich dream life, we may find that our dreams become more frequent, vivid, and meaningful. We may experience a greater sense of connection to our subconscious mind and a deeper understanding of ourselves and our place in the world. We may also discover hidden talents, tap into our intuition, and find guidance on our life path.

The art of dreaming is a journey of self-discovery, a process of unfolding and awakening to the boundless potential that lies within us. By embracing the power of our dreams, we can transform our lives and create a more meaningful and fulfilling existence. So let us embrace the art of dreaming, and allow our dreams to guide us towards a brighter future.

▷▷▷

Your dreams are a unique expression of your individuality. Embrace their quirks and peculiarities, and you will discover a deeper understanding of yourself and your place in the world.

NINETEEN

THE DREAM THERAPIST: USING YOUR DREAMS FOR HEALING AND GROWTH.

Within the ethereal landscape of our dreams, a profound potential for healing and growth awaits. Dreams, often dismissed as mere figments of our imagination, are in fact a potent tool for exploring the depths of our subconscious and unlocking the secrets that lie within. The Dream Therapist, a guide and interpreter of this nocturnal realm, can help us navigate the intricate pathways of our dreams, leading us towards self-discovery, emotional healing, and personal transformation.

Since ancient times, dreams have been revered as a source of wisdom and guidance. Shamans, oracles, and healers across cultures have recognized the power of dreams to reveal hidden truths and offer solutions to life's challenges. In modern psychology, dream therapy has emerged as a valuable tool for understanding and addressing a wide range of psychological and emotional issues.

At its core, dream therapy is based on the premise that dreams are a reflection of our innermost selves. They are a symbolic language through which our subconscious communicates with us, expressing our deepest fears, desires, and unresolved conflicts. By paying attention to the symbols, emotions, and themes that appear in our dreams, we can gain valuable insights into our waking lives.

The Dream Therapist serves as a guide and interpreter on this journey of self-discovery. They provide a safe and supportive space for us to explore our dreams, to decipher their hidden meanings, and to integrate their messages into our waking lives. Through a variety of techniques, such as dream journaling, dream incubation, and active imagination, the Dream Therapist can help us to unlock the healing potential of our dreams.

Dream journaling is a powerful tool for capturing and preserving the ephemeral nature of dreams. By recording our dreams upon waking, we can create a record of our nocturnal journeys and uncover patterns and themes that may not be immediately apparent. The Dream Therapist can help us to analyze these patterns and identify recurring symbols or motifs that may hold significant meaning for us.

Dream incubation is another valuable technique that the Dream Therapist may employ. This involves setting an intention before bed to dream about a specific topic or issue. By focusing our minds on a particular question or problem before we sleep, we can increase the likelihood of receiving guidance or insights in our dreams. For example, a person struggling with anxiety may set an intention to dream about their fears, allowing them to confront and process these emotions in a safe and supportive environment.

Active imagination is a technique that involves consciously engaging with the characters and symbols in our dreams. This can be done through writing, drawing, or even acting out the dream scenario. By actively interacting with our dreams, we can deepen our understanding of their meaning and significance. The Dream Therapist can guide us through this process, helping us to access the emotions and memories associated with our dreams.

Through dream therapy, we can gain a deeper understanding of ourselves and our relationships. We can identify and address unresolved conflicts, heal from past traumas, and develop healthier coping mechanisms. We can also discover hidden talents, tap into our intuition, and find guidance on our life path.

The Dream Therapist can also help us to understand and address recurring nightmares. Nightmares are often a manifestation of our deepest fears and anxieties. By working with a Dream Therapist to explore the meaning of our nightmares, we can begin to confront and overcome these fears.

Dream therapy is a powerful tool for personal growth and transformation. It offers a unique opportunity to delve into the depths of our subconscious and unlock the secrets that lie within. By working with a skilled and compassionate Dream Therapist, we can harness the healing power of our dreams and create a more fulfilling and meaningful life.

ﬡﬡﬡ

Dreams are not just for nighttime; they can be a source of inspiration and guidance throughout your day. By carrying the wisdom of your dreams with you, you can navigate life's challenges with greater confidence and clarity.

TWENTY

THE LUCID DREAMER: AWAKENING TO YOUR DREAMS.

In the realm of dreams, a hidden power lies dormant within each of us—the ability to become aware that we are dreaming while still asleep. This extraordinary phenomenon, known as lucid dreaming, opens up a world of infinite possibilities, allowing us to consciously explore and shape the dreamscape, to confront our fears and anxieties, to unleash our creativity, and to embark on fantastical adventures that defy the laws of reality.

Lucid dreaming is not a new concept. It has been practiced and documented for centuries in various cultures around the world. Ancient Tibetan Buddhists, for example, developed intricate techniques for inducing lucid dreams as part of their spiritual practices.

In modern times, scientific research has begun to shed light on the neurological mechanisms underlying lucid dreaming, confirming its validity as a real and measurable phenomenon.

At its core, lucid dreaming is a state of heightened awareness within the dream state. It is a moment of awakening within the dream itself, a realization that we are not merely passive observers, but active participants in the unfolding narrative. This awareness empowers us to take control of our dreams, to explore their limitless possibilities, and to harness their transformative power.

The benefits of lucid dreaming are vast and varied. For some, lucid dreaming offers a thrilling escape from the mundane realities of waking life. It provides a playground where we can indulge in our wildest fantasies, explore exotic locations, and interact with fantastical creatures.

For others, lucid dreaming is a powerful tool for personal growth and self-discovery. It allows us to confront our fears and anxieties in a safe and controlled environment, to rehearse for challenging situations, and to explore our creative potential.

Lucid dreaming can also be used for therapeutic purposes. By consciously engaging with the content of our dreams, we can gain valuable insights into our subconscious thoughts and emotions. We can identify and address unresolved conflicts, heal from past traumas, and develop healthier coping mechanisms.

Lucid dreaming has been used to treat nightmares, phobias, and post-traumatic stress disorder, offering a unique and effective approach to psychological healing.

But how does one become a lucid dreamer? While some people seem to experience lucid dreams spontaneously, for most of us, it requires practice and dedication. There are many techniques for inducing lucid dreams, each with its own advantages and drawbacks.

One common technique is reality testing. This involves periodically checking throughout the day to see if you are awake or dreaming. By establishing a habit of reality testing, you can train your mind to carry this awareness into the dream state, leading to increased lucidity.

Another technique is dream journaling. By recording our dreams upon waking, we can increase our awareness of their content and recurring patterns. This awareness can then be used to trigger lucidity within the dream itself. For example, if you notice that you often dream of flying, you can make a mental note to check if you are dreaming the next time you find yourself airborne.

Meditation and mindfulness practices can also be beneficial for cultivating lucid dreaming. By quieting the mind and focusing on the present moment, we can increase our awareness of our internal states and our thoughts and emotions. This heightened awareness can then be carried into the dream state, leading to greater lucidity.

There are also various technological tools available to aid in lucid dreaming. These include specialized sleep masks that detect REM sleep and provide auditory or visual cues to induce lucidity, as well as smartphone apps that offer guided meditations and dream journaling features.

While lucid dreaming can be a powerful tool for personal growth and transformation, it is important to approach it with caution and respect. Dreams are a complex and often unpredictable phenomenon, and there is always a risk of encountering disturbing or unsettling content.

It is important to remember that lucid dreaming is not a substitute for professional therapy, and if you are struggling with significant emotional or psychological issues, it is important to seek help from a qualified healthcare provider.

For those who are willing to explore the depths of their subconscious, lucid dreaming offers a gateway to a world of infinite possibilities. It is a journey of self-discovery, a chance to confront our fears, to unleash our creativity, and to awaken to the full potential of our dreams.

ᗰᗰᗰ

In the vast landscape of your dreams, you are the explorer, the creator, and the hero. Embrace the adventure, and let your dreams guide you towards a more vibrant, meaningful, and fulfilling life.

TWENTY-ONE
SUMMARY

Dreams, those enigmatic tapestries woven in the loom of our sleeping minds, hold a profound power within them. They are not mere fleeting illusions, but a language through which our subconscious communicates with us, offering insights into our deepest desires, fears, and unresolved conflicts. By deciphering the whispers of the night, we can unlock a world of wisdom, healing, and personal growth.

This comprehensive guide has delved into the many facets of the dream world, providing you with tools and knowledge to navigate its intricate landscapes. We began by acknowledging the mystery and allure of dreams, exploring their historical significance and the myriad ways they have been interpreted across cultures and time periods.

We delved into the concept of the Dream Dictionary, a repository of common dream symbols and their potential meanings. We emphasized that dream interpretation is a personal journey, and that the same symbol can hold different significance for different individuals. However, by understanding the common language of dreams, we can begin to decipher the messages our subconscious is trying to convey.

The Dreamer's Handbook offered practical guidance on interpreting dreams, highlighting the importance of dream journaling as a tool for capturing and reflecting upon our nocturnal adventures. We explored various techniques for decoding dream symbols, including free association, active imagination, and dream re-entry. By actively engaging with our dreams, we can uncover hidden truths about ourselves and our lives.

The Dreamer's Compass showed us how dreams can guide us on our life path, acting as an internal compass pointing us towards our true purpose and passions. We learned to recognize recurring symbols and themes in our dreams as potential signposts, directing us towards areas of our lives that require attention or exploration.

We ventured beyond the boundaries of reality, journeying through the diverse landscapes of our dreams. We encountered fantastical creatures, revisited cherished memories, and confronted our deepest fears. These dream experiences, while often surreal and illogical, can offer profound insights into our subconscious minds and our waking lives.

The power of dreams extends beyond mere entertainment or self-discovery. Dreams can also be a catalyst for healing and growth. The Dream Therapist, a skilled guide and interpreter of the dream world, can help us to navigate the complexities of our dreams and unlock their therapeutic potential. By confronting our fears, processing unresolved emotions, and integrating dream insights into our waking lives, we can experience profound healing and transformation.

We explored the art of dreaming, recognizing that a rich and vibrant dream life can be cultivated through intention and practice. By incorporating techniques such as dream incubation, lucid dreaming, and creative expression, we can deepen our connection to our dreams and unlock their full potential.

The Dreamer's Journal served as a constant companion on this journey, providing a safe space to record our dreams, track our progress, and explore the depths of our subconscious. We emphasized the importance of maintaining a consistent practice of dream journaling, as it allows us to identify recurring patterns, symbols, and themes that can offer valuable insights into our lives.

In conclusion, this comprehensive guide has equipped you with the tools and knowledge you need to embark on your own journey of dream exploration. By embracing the power of your dreams, you can unlock a world of wisdom, healing, and personal growth. Remember, the journey is just as important as the destination. So let your curiosity guide you, trust your intuition, and allow your dreams to illuminate your path.

ᗡᗡᗡ

Citation And References

This book represents the culmination of extensive research and meticulous analysis, incorporating a diverse range of sources, including numerous books, scholarly studies, and personal experiences. Additionally, I have scoured various websites to gather relevant information and data essential for the compilation of this work. I have taken every precaution to ensure the accuracy of the information presented and have diligently cited all sources to acknowledge their contributions.

Despite these efforts, the possibility of inadvertent errors remains. I deeply value the insights of my readers and appreciate any feedback that can help identify and rectify such inaccuracies. I encourage you to bring any discrepancies to my attention.

Your feedback is not only welcome but crucial, as it will aid in correcting current editions and enhancing the content of future ones. I am committed to maintaining the highest standards of accuracy and reliability in my work and thank you for your support and understanding.

Additionally, I firmly uphold the principle of freedom of speech and expression as guaranteed under Article 19(1)(a) of the Constitution of India, and I respect the diverse viewpoints and expressions of all readers.

ﮒﮒﮒ

Other Books Of The Author

1. Empowering Minds: A Journey into Women's Self-Discovery and Power
2. The Dynamics of Motivation: Catalyzing Thought into Action
3. Meditation and Mental Well Being: The Path to Inner Peace and Clarity
4. The Psychology of Child Education: Nurturing Future Generations
5. Ethical Enlightenment: A Modern Guide to Living with Integrity
6. Voices of Empowerment: Stories of Women Rising Against Odds
7. Social Psychology in Everyday Life: Understanding Human Connections
8. The Essence of Motivational Speaking: Inspiring Change in Others
9. Balancing Acts: Women, Work, and the Will to Lead
10. Guiding with Grace: Raising Children with Compassion and Awareness
11. The Power of Positive Aging: Embracing Life After Fifty
12. Building Resilient Communities: Social Work in Action
13. The Ethical Educator: Principles for Teaching and Learning
14. From Insight to Impact: Social Psychology for a Better World
15. The Ethics of Empathy: A Guide to Ethical Living
16. The Science of Empowering the Self: Navigating Life's Challenges with Psychological Wisdom
17. The Mindful Conscious Leader: Meditation Techniques for Modern Management
18. Pioneering Spirit: Women's Pathways to Leadership and Empowerment
19. Feeling to Healing: The Role of Emotional Intelligence in Child Development
20. Transformative Talks and Words of Inspiration: Insights into Motivational Oratory

21. Green Ethics: A Path to Sustainable Living
22. Spiritual Integrity: Navigating Life with Moral Compassion
23. Clean Living, Clean Society: The Ethics of Cleanliness
24. Patriotic Spirits: Building a Nation on Positive Attitudes
25. Innovative Integrity & Vibrant Visions: The Ethical and Entrepreneurial Spirit of Gujarat
26. Youthful Visions, Endless Possibilities: Inspiring Ethics and Motivation in Children
27. Living Your Legacy: How to Motivate Others by Living Your Values
28. Secret of Healing Conversations: Ethical Practices in Counselling and Therapy
29. Creative Kindness: Crafting a Life of Compassion and Creativity
30. The Power of Appreciation: How Gratitude Can Transform Your Relationships
31. Bhagavad-Gita: Messages
32. Science of Art: The New Frontier of Fashion Modernism
33. Vivekananda's Virtues: A Blueprint for Modern Living
34. Empower Her: Navigating the Path to Women's Entrepreneurship
35. The Boundless Classroom: Innovations in Global Education
36. The Language of Leadership: Communicating with Authenticity and Impact
37. The Warrior's Mantra: Deciphering the Hanuman Chalisa
38. Echoes of Empathy: Transformative Stories of Social Service
39. Artful Living: Cultivating Creativity in Your Daily Routine
40. Finding Your Why: Discovering Your Passions and Charting Your Course
41. The Role of Social Media in Shaping Self-Esteem and Interpersonal Relationships among Adolescents
42. Karma's Tapestry: Weaving a Life of Selfless Service
43. Altruistic Alchemy: Transforming Lives Through Giving
44. The Blueprint of Pro-Activeness and Productivity: Crafting Habits for Success
45. The Simplicity with Grounded Wisdom: Embracing Authenticity

in a Complex World

46. Secret of Solopreneur's Odyssey: Navigating the Path to Self-Employment

47. Exploring Tapestry of Peace: Global Perspectives on Harmony

48. The Art and Actions of Connection: Mastering Communication for Impact

49. She Governs and at the Helm: Strategies for Political Empowerment

50. Rising Above and Rising with Grace: A Woman's Roadmap to Career Mastery

51. The Effect of Networking & Connectedness: Building Strategic Alliances for Women

52. Beyond his Barriers: Women Thriving in Male-Dominated Fields

53. Secret of Inner Compass: Navigating Life with Intuition

54. Creative & Pro-Active Muses: A Celebration of Women in the Arts

55. Unburdened: The Art of Releasing the Past

56. Amplified Voices: Speeches of Women that Astonished the World

57. Secret of Manifesting Dreams: A Woman's Guide to Intentional Living

58. Ethics and Value Based Education: Reimagining Japan's School System

59. The Moral Compass Curriculum: A Holistic Approach

60. Tech with Heart: Integrating Ethics into Digital Learning

61. Honoring Virtue: Recognizing Ethical Excellence in Education

62. Raising Good Humans: A Guide to Character Development

63. The Spark Within: Nurturing Creativity in Children

64. The Teenager Whisperer: Navigating Adolescence with Grace

65. Igniting a Passion for Learning: Inspiring Lifelong Curiosity

66. The Habit Lab: Cultivating Positive Behaviors in Children

67. Seeds of Empathy: Fostering Compassion in Young Hearts

68. The Reading Revolution: Inspiring a Love of Books in Children

69. The Learning Brain: Unlocking the Secrets of Student Success

70. Teaching for All: Differentiated Instruction Strategies

71. The Time Alchemist: Mastering Time Management for Peak Performance

72. The Resilience Factor: Transforming Setbacks into Stepping Stones

73. The Healing Touch of Nature: An Introduction to Naturopathy

74. Echoes of the Past: Healing Through Past Life Regression

75. The Spiritual Healer's Handbook: Exploring Energy Medicine

76. Crystal Clarity: Unveiling the Power of Gemstones

77. The Dream Weaver's Guide: Decoding the Language of Dreams

78. Emotional Alchemy: Transforming Pain into Power

79. Sonic Serenity: Harnessing Sound for Stress Relief

80. The Entrepreneur's Playbook: Launching Your Business with Confidence

81. Productivity Unleashed: Time Management Strategies for Entrepreneurs

82. The Problem Solver's Toolkit: Creative Solutions for Business Challenges

83. The Future is Now: Emerging Trends in Business

84. The Curious Explorer: A Child's Guide to Scientific Discovery

85. Digital Pioneers: Empowering Kids in the Tech World

86. The Young Philosopher's Guide: Exploring Life's Big Questions

87. Finding Your Voice: Communication Skills for Confident Kids

88. Nature's Playground: A Child's Guide to Outdoor Adventure

89. Growing a Greener Tomorrow: A Guide to Tree Planting & Conservation

90. Driving with Purpose: Ethical Choices on the Road

91. The Healing Touch: Cultivating Compassion in Healthcare

92. Navigating the Digital Landscape: Ethics in the Age of Social Media

93. The Ethical Closet: A Guide to Sustainable Fashion

94. The Mindful Voyager: Sustainable Travel Practices

95. The Feminine Divine: Honoring the Goddesses of India

96. Sacred Sounds: Chanting Your Way to Inner Peace

97. The Yoga Path: Uniting with the Divine Within

98. Rites of Passage: Creating Meaningful Ceremonies

99. The Chakra System: A Map of Inner Transformation

100. Spiritual Sangha: Finding Community through Satsang and

Bhajan

101. Pilgrimage of the Soul: Spiritual Journeys in India

❦❦❦

Contact

Dr. Minakshi Bansal
Social Activist
Ahmedabad, Gujarat, Bharat
minakshiindiag20@yahoo.com

❦❦❦

|| LOKAHA SAMASTHAHA SUKHINO BHAVANTU ||